The BestFit

Performance Based, Behavioural & Cognitive Interview Tools

BY ROCHELLE A. R. JAMES

The BestFit

Performance Based, Behavioural &
Cognitive Interview Tools

The BestFit

Performance Based, Behavioural &
Cognitive Interview Tools

Rochelle A. R. James

ISBNs
978-976-96331-0-0 (paperback)
978-976-96331-1-7 (eBook)

Published June 2019 by Rochelle Analecia Reid James
Book designed by Ronaldo Russell

Limited Liability/Disclaimer of Warranty
While the author has used her best efforts in preparing this book, she makes no representations, guarantees or warranties with respect to the accuracy or completeness of the contents of this book and disclaims any such warranties implied. The advice, tools and strategies contained in this book may not be suitable for your situation. The author shall not be liable for any loss of profit or any other commercial damages, including but not limited to special incidental, consequential, or other damages.

Publication Data
Name: Rochelle Analecia Reid James
Title: BESTFIT: PERFORMANCE BASED, BEHAVIOURAL & COGNITIVE INTERVIEW TOOLS
Subject: Human Resource, Recruitment and Personnel Management
Printed in Kingston, Jamaica

ISBNs
978-976-96331-0-0 (paperback)
978-976-96331-1-7 (eBook)

Disclaimer
Considerable care has been taken to ensure this document is both accurate and relevant. However the author provides no guarantees concerning the accuracy, completeness or relevance of the contents of this book to your organization.

These tools and techniques are meant to be shared. As you share them share the credit. Remember to cite your source.

Dedication

A community of people supported the knowledge shared in this book and I honor them all.

God
without Him the possible would be impossible.

Rik
the one who encouraged me to write,

the one who encourages me to excel.

Mommy, Daddy & Ryan
the ones who continue to encourage me to change the world.

Sheryll & Tania
the ones who encouraged me to share

my creativity by writing this book.

"You can't let people and their lack of integrity stop you from sharing knowledge" (said by: Sheryll Brown)
"Why would you think you can't do it? Of course you can!"

(said by: Tania McDonald-Tomlinson)

Sheree, Gina, Charmaine, Ramsay & Blaine
the ones who continue to support me on my journey.

Foreword

I am relatively new to the field of Human Resource Management; however I've been a "customer" of HR for my entire professional career having transitioned from a Summer Worker to an HR Director over the course of the past 24 years, 15 roles, 9 companies and 6 countries. Specifically, I've been in some form of leadership for the last eight (8) years, going through the entire employee lifecycle myself and with my teams. I used to think my work was hard until I entered leadership; then I realized the work itself was easy, but the people could make the work hard. Leaders and scholars talk all the time about Tuckman's three (3) stages of Team Development; forming, storming and norming… but many times we forget that there is an initial phase for all of us as employees: recruitment! This could arguably be the most important determining factor for any team's success. How did this person get into the organization, into your Division or Unit, on your team? What was the criteria used for their selection? Do his or her values align with those of your organization? Did anyone check the individual's behavior and mental capacity (psychometrics) to see if he or she would "fit" with the other persons on your team? All these questions and more will influence how difficult the stages will be for your team to traverse.

In 2019, many companies are still using archaic interview methods with no greater aim than to see how well dressed and well-spoken their candidates are and how they react to tough, complicated questions. I've been fortunate enough to see and participate in a variety of interview techniques and have come to realise that as the business environments change and workforces change, our methods of recruitment HAVE TO CHANGE.

That's why I'm excited about the methodology Rochelle has chosen to pursue in this text, as it challenges Human Resource practitioners to think and operate differently in their interviews and overall recruitment processes. It challenges leaders to look at their requirements differently and to transform their needs and yet remain aligned with the changing needs of their business.

I've known Rochelle for just over three (3) years, and for the past year I've worked closely with her as a mentor and colleague in the field of Human Resources. Her passion for people-development and her overall radical approach to life and relationships shine through in the R3 technique and you are in for an interesting journey in this book. You will question your pre-existing beliefs about interview methods and the people you are interviewing, and be challenged to bring a new perspective to the interview table.

Gina Tomlinson- Williams
Human Resource Director
Jamaica Public Service Company Limited

Preface

I am sorry but we decided to go with another candidate who was a better fit for the role." If you have ever had to read those words after a job interview you believed you aced, then I assure you it was even harder for the recruiter who had to send that email. I have been on both sides, as the recruiter who had to send that email and the rejected candidate who had to read it, all in the same week. That was one of the hardest weeks of my life.

The experience forced me to think seriously about how I recruit candidates. Does each candidate know that what I am looking for is not the most qualified or experienced person for the job, but someone who is the 'bestfit'? What does it mean to be the bestfit and why wasn't I the bestfit? Being a recruiter myself did not make answering these questions any easier, but it led me to a solution. I was able to develop an interviewing technique that supported both the interviewer and the interviewee. This technique was designed to help both to identify if the interviewee was the "BESTFIT" for the particular role in the organisation.

Contents

The BestFit

Definition

The Most suitable candidate to work in the role, the department and the company for which he/she is being hired.

Introduction

Dave Ulrich, partner at strategic HR transformation and leadership development giant RBL Group, in the forward to the Human Resource Body of Knowledge wrote that "Human Resource matters more than ever in the value creation process" (Reed, 2017). From Ulrich's writings we learn that current Human Resource insights are more about how businesses make hiring, training or compensation decisions and how these decisions deliver value to employees and customers. Recruitment plays a crucial role in delivering value to the business. This is why I take recruitment so seriously. I believe each candidate I employ is joining my family and each 'bestfit' hire is my value added contribution to the business. This person is a new piece of a giant puzzle for which, as the recruiter, I have been tasked to get the right fit.

Most employees spend in excess of eight (8) hours per day with each other; that is one third (1/3) of your day spent away from your biological family. Without your consent, your co-workers are your extended family and the experiences you have at work with them will impact your day. This means that if an employee adds negativity to the work space then it may affect both your work and home life. Each new employee you add to the company should bring positive energy or be able to quell any existing negative energy. Hence the decision to recruit the right person who fits in with the personality and employee brand of your organization is crucial. Twenty-first (21st) century companies should focus on evaluating potential employees through the use of assessment tools that reflect the company's brand and offer clear insight into the candidate they are recruiting.

Current literature on behavioral interviews indicates that the logic behind this interviewing technique is: your behavior in the past reflects and predicts how you will behave in the future. So the interviewer will ask questions that force the candidate to use the STAR (Specific situation, Task, Action, and Result) technique in responding, to bring out that behavior. While this can reveal several things it is one dimensional and eliminates candidates with little experience but high potential or those who have changed over time. As people we evolve and grow so our interviews should be designed to account for that growth and evolution. This means the interview process should not only account for the candidate's past performance, but predict their future potential. As a recruiter would you engage a candidate with very high potential, but limited relevant experience, someone who checks every box except the experience box? If the answer is yes, then this means you value the potential and suitability of a candidate. This means finding the 'BESTFIT' is important to you. If the answer is no, this means an experienced candidate is more important to you and maybe this book is not for you.

Old interviewing techniques (e.g. asking questions like 'Where do you see yourself in 5 years?') have hacks or simple responses that can be found with one key stroke. These 'tricks' of the trade for interviewees offer them tools and techniques for giving the best response. The idea of giving the best response or the right answer turns the interview into a test and not a "getting to know you" experience. The belief that there is a right or wrong answer turns the candidate into a well-rehearsed zombie during the interview. The interview is not a test, it should be more like a first date where the interviewers get to know the interviewee and assess if he/she is the "BESTFIT" for the role being considered.

To achieve this "BESTFIT" the selection process must be transformed. This book will explore what three dimensional (3D) interviews are, how they can be used as a social psychology tool and the benefits to be derived when combined with the R3 technique. As you continue to read, it will become apparent that the R3 technique, as a methodology, allows the recruiter to carry out a full scan of the candidate's past, present and future state (potential, attitude and aptitude). Employing these techniques, through the use of interview activities, add depth to the interviewing process. This book will take you through a series of interviewing tools to use and add to your recruitment strategy.

My colleagues and I have used the tools in this book to recruit for both technical and non-technical vacancies. Those participating in the interview process (panelists, successful candidates and unsuccessful candidates) have all lauded the technique.

Photo of Thomas Edison
(Classic Chicago Magazine)

EDISON QUESTIONS STIR UP A STORM

"Victims" of Test Say Only "a Walking Encyclopedia" Could Answer Questionnaire.

OFFICIAL LIST A SECRET

But Man Who Remembers 141 Questions Tells What They Were and Calls Them Silly.

Thomas A. Edison's examination questions for college graduates seeking employment as executives in his plant and the inventor's unfavorable opinion of college men because they couldn't answer the questions, have evoked many protests, both from "victims" of the examination and others. The general tenor of the comments is that the questions only could be answered by a walking encyclopedia and are a test of a man's memory and store of miscellaneous information, rather than of his knowledge, reasoning power or intelligence.

Several letters commenting indignantly upon the test have been received by THE NEW YORK TIMES. A typical one suggests that it was "not a Tom Edison but a Tom Foolery test." Another says that even a college graduate is a human being and is interested in other things besides the depth of the ocean, while a third accuses Mr. Edison of having been guilty of that conspicuous human frailty against which Socrates gave warning: Belief that because he knows one thing well, he knows all things well.

Refuses to Make Questions Public.

An effort was made to get from Mr. Edison or his representatives both a reply to the critics and an authentic list of the questions. Mr. Edison was home because of a slight cold and would not talk. H. W. Meadowcroft, Mr. Edison's secretary, refused to make the questions public on the ground that future applicants would be enabled to cram for the examinations.

cently measured and found to be of enormous size?

What large river in the United States is it that flows from south to north?

Where are the Straits of Messina?

In what country are earthquakes frequent?

What mountain is the highest in the world?

Where do we import cork from?

Name six big business men in the United States.

Who is called the father of railways?

Where was Lincoln born?

Who stated the following: "Fourscore and seven years ago," &c.?

What business do you like best?

Are you experienced in any of the following: Salesmanship, clerk, stenography, bookkeeping?

Name a few kinds of wood used in making furniture, and the highest priced?

What kind of wood is the lightest?

What kind of wood is the heaviest?

Of what kind of wood are axe handles made?

Of what kind of wood are kerosene barrels made?

What part of Germany do we get toys from?

What States bound West Virginia?

Where do we get peanuts from?

What is the capital of Alabama?

Who wrote the "Star-Spangled Banner"?

Who wrote "Home, Sweet Home"?

Who composed "Il Trovatore"?

Who was Cleopatra?

Where are condors to be found?

What voltage is used on street cars?

Who discovered the law of gravitation?

What cereal is used all over the world?

Where is the Assuan Dam?

What country produces the most nickel?

What is the distance between the earth and the sun?

Who invented photography?

Where do we get wool from?

What is felt?

What States produce phosphates?

Why is cast iron called pig iron?

Name three principal acids?

Name three principal alkalis?

Name three powerful poisons?

Who discovered radium?

Who discovered the X-ray?

What is the weight of air in a room 20x30x10?

Where is platinum found?

With what metal is platinum associated when found?

How is sulphuric acid made?

Who discovered how to vulcanize rubber?

Where do we get sulphur from?

Where do we import rubber from?

Who invented the cotton gin?

What is the price of 12 grs. of gold?

What is vulcanite and how made?

What is glucose and how made?

What is the difference between anthracite and bituminous coal?

Where do we get benzol from?

Of what is glass made?

How is window glass made?

What is porcelain?

What kind of a machine is used in cutting the facets on diamonds?

What country makes the best optical lenses and what city?

Where do we get borax from?

What is a foot pound?

"The whole point of the test would be lost if its contents were published," Mr. Meadowcroft said. "I will say, however, that it covers pretty thoroughly a man's supply of general information. Mr. Edison originated the questionnaire three or four months ago and is well satisfied with the results. Only some thirty of the several hundred applicants have managed to pass the test, it is true, but those who did and thus became inspectors of the factory have made good in every case. The plan is to advance those men to executive and administrative positions if their future progress is satisfactory."

Though the official list remained a carefully guarded secret, known in its entirety only to Mr. Edison, Mr. Meadowcroft and a clerk, 141 of the questions were sent to THE TIMES yesterday by Charles Hansen, an unsuccessful candidate. No person who takes the examination is allowed to write down the questions or make notes of them, so Mr. Hansen's list is from memory and he makes no pretense of giving more than the substance and purport of the queries. The attitude of Mr. Edison and his aids made verification impossible.

Here Is Hansen's List.

This is the list:

What countries bound France?

Where is the River Volga?

What country and city produce the finest china?

Where does the finest cotton grow?

What country consumed the most tea before the war?

What city in the United States is noted for its laundry machine making?

What city is the fur centre in the United States?

Can you play any musical instrument?

What country is the greatest textile producer?

Is Australia larger than Greenland in area?

Where is Copenhagen?

Where is Spitzbergen?

In what country other than Australia are kangaroos found?

What telescope is the largest in the world?

Who was Bessemer and what did he do?

Where do we get prunes from?

How many States in the Union?

Who was Paul Revere?

Who was Hancock?

Who was Plutarch?

Who was Hannibal?

Who was Danton?

Who was Solon?

Who was Frances Marion?

Who was Leonidas?

Where did we get Louisiana from?

Who was Pizarro?

Who was Bolivar?

What war material did Chile export to the Allies during the war?

Where does the most coffee come from?

Calls Examination Silly.

Mr. Hansen calls attention to the fact that he was able to remember so nearly all the questions, remarks that that is "not so bad for an ignorant college graduate," expresses the opinion that the examination is more appropriate for a high school boy than a college man, and says:

"I want you and the public to judge whether a full blooded man who has been out of college and out in the business world for the past ten years could average 50 per cent. on this silly examination."

Another letter received yesterday described the experience of a man who answered Mr. Edison's advertisement for a production engineer, was told that his qualifications were satisfactory and then was required to answer a questionnaire, after which he was to have had a personal interview with the inventor.

"I finally completed my answers to the sixty or more questions," he writes. "During this time Mr. Edison paced back and forth, irritably demanding why certain results were not being obtained in his factory and denouncing what he termed bone-headed moves on the part of his executives, while the latter shouted their excuses into his deaf ears. My written answers were given to him, and after a few moments of waiting I was told I had failed and was 'given the air' with the other fellows who had also failed.

Answers Safest in Textbooks.

"Aside from several silly catch questions, the majority were ones embracing formulas that are always safest when left in standard textbooks. Any attempt to memorize formulas and little used specifications is, without doubt, disastrous, and may be compared to a man operating a large business by his memory rather than by bookkeeping.

"Some of the questions were: 'What is a Chinese windlass?' If six brick were placed on a glass plate, would it require more effort to move them if placed side by side or on top of one another?' If a ball weighing one pound is dropped from a height of one foot on an anvil what force in pounds would it create when striking the anvil?' 'What pinch pressure at the driving wheels does a 25-ton locomotive require when drawing a load of 100 tons on level track?'"

The History of The Interview Process

It is not clear when the practice of conducting employment interviews became common practice; however it can be traced back to inventor of the light bulb, Thomas Edison. Historical accounts note that Edison used interviews to select the ideal candidate to work with him on his inventions. By using 150 questions (called a pre-employment test) Edison evaluated their knowledge and suitability to fit the role of assistant. His methodology was seen as novel and many other inventors and industry leaders began using the same technique to select their best fit employees. Dubbed the "Edison test" by the New York Times this piece of history is central to the history of recruitment practices and interviewing techniques. On May 11, 1921 the New York Times published an article, (Edison Questions Stir Up A Storm, 1921) in which it described the test takers as Edison's victims. The article also recounted a quote from one test taker who described the test and its questions to be silly. (When I first tested one of my cognitive tools, the candidate scoffed at it and said it was a waste of time. The results showed that he was unfit for the role and time later confirmed what the tool had revealed).

Associate Editor and management columnist with the Financial Times, Lucy Kellaway, has jokingly posited an alternative account of the history of interviews. Lucy postulates that the first job interview was conducted by Jesus in the book of John chapter 1 verse 38 when He was recruiting disciples and asked them "What do you seek?" (Kellaway, 2012). Whichever historical account you accept as true the reality is that the techniques used to conduct interviews have changed over time.

In the 1990s, the techniques heavily emphasized skills, experience and qualifications. A Master's degree was not commonplace and working with the same employer for decades was the trend. During this time the questions focused on confirming loyalty and technical competence. Some well-known sample questions include:

Tell me about yourself. ...
Why should we hire you? ...
What is your greatest strength? ...
What is your greatest weakness? ...

Questions asked were very technical or were framed as brain teasers. The interview room was a tense space of drills.

Now, in the nineteenth year of the 2000's the purpose of the interview has changed. The focus is not just on the candidate impressing the employer; instead it is for the employer to impress the candidate as well. During the interview the potential employer and potential employee have the opportunity to learn more about each other and decide if the candidate and the role are a BESTFIT for each other. Questions should be heavily focused on pulling out behaviours as proof points of the candidate's potential, based on past successes.

Tara de Jonge, a Human Resource Business Partner at Roche Diagnostics (a research-based healthcare company) wrote an article in 2015 entitled "Getting with the times, Giving Old-School Interview Questions a Modern Twist" (Jonge, 2015). Tara offered guidance on how to modernize old fashioned interview questions to make them behavioural. Here are my two favorites:

This interviewing practice has since evolved into the model of interviews with which we are most familiar (performance based & behavioural interviews). However this model is still going through changes.

What are Interview Techniques?

A part of the journey towards identifying your ideal candidate is determining which interview technique you (the recruiter) will use. An interview technique is the strategy, method or approach a recruiter takes when conducting a face to face meeting with a candidate. The technique is demonstrated in the question and answer (Q&A) portion of the interview. Your interview technique is the HIT in the questions you ask:

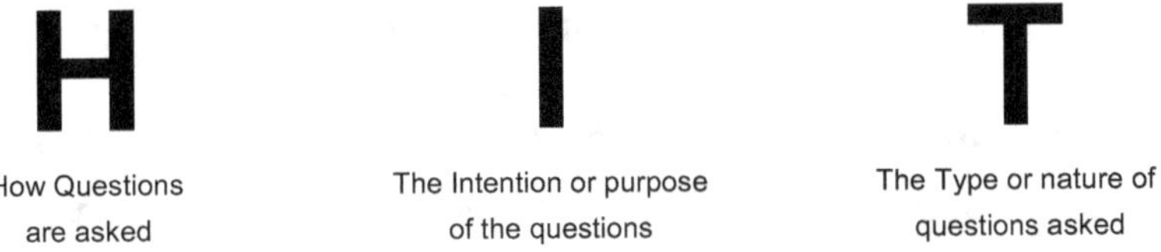

The abbreviation HIT is a simplification of the interview design. How the interviewer designs the interview experience (the technique) usually follows any one or a combination of five (5) set styles – Five Interview Techniques – that are usually incorporated with the standard interview process flow.

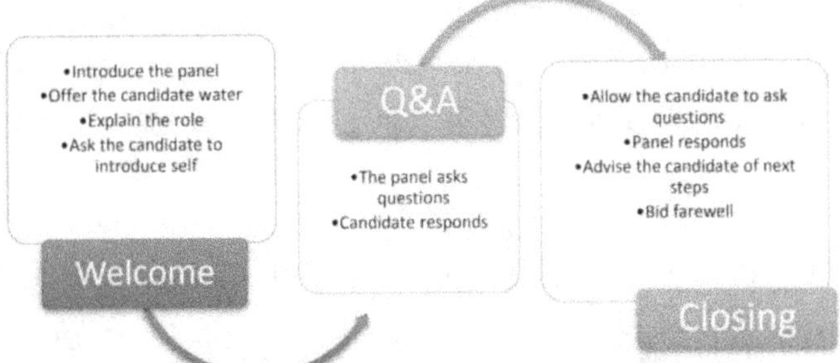

Fig. 1.0 – Standard Interview Process Flow

These five (5) known interview techniques are: Behavioural Interview, Competency-based Interview, Brain Teaser Technique and Dumb Question Technique.

Top 5 Interview Techniques

Behavioral Interview Technique - the interviewer asks the applicant how he or she handled a particular situation in the past (Society of Human Resource Management)

Competency-based Interview Technique - the interviewer asks questions focused on the skills needed for the position; the candidate is measured against the job-related skills as the main criteria (Society of Human Resource Management)

Situational Interview Technique – the interviewer shares a hypothetical scenario, case or event with the candidate then asks the candidate to provide specific examples of how he/she would respond to the given scenario. The questions focus on his/ her past experiences, behaviors, knowledge, skills and abilities. (Society of Human Resource Management)

Brainteaser Technique (Case questions) – the interviewer asks simple or mundane problem-solving questions that are designed to draw out how someone would work and think through a simple problem: "how many traffic lights are in Los Angeles?" (Workable, 2015)

Dumb Questions Technique – the interviewer asks questions intended to test the candidate's ability to think on their feet. They often just test people's patience and good humor: "What kind of animal would you like to be? (Workable, 2015)

Interview Techniques For Finding The BestFit

According to entrepreneurial journalist Nina Wasserman's article on www.inc.com (entitled "A Closer Look at Behavior-Based Interviewing") the practice of using "Behavior-Based Interviewing" dates back to 1970 when a company called Behavioral Technology (Wasserman, 2000) designed behaviour based questions in response to the changing job market and the increased demand for highly skilled employees.

The terms "Behavioural Interviews", "Behaviour-Based interviews" and "Performance Based interviews" are used inter-changeably and in some cases they are used to categorize three (3) distinct interviewing models. There are three (3) types of interviewing techniques: Behavioural, Performance Based and Cognitive.

Behavioural Interviews

Your past actions (behaviours) are the best
predictors of future performance

A behavioural interview is a modern technique where employers assess a candidate's suitability by asking a series of questions that help to reveal how the candidate has acted or will act in specific employment-related scenarios.

This technique takes into account the combination of the candidate's personal and professional life. The philosophy behind this concept is if the candidate is organized at home then, this individual will be organized at work. Companies want to hire the complete person. These questions tend to be more relaxed and would appear unrelated to the functions of the job; however they reveal the candidate's suitability as the right fit for the culture of the organization.

Performance Based Interviews

Your past performance is the best predictor of
future performance

The focus of this technique is on the candidate as a professional. The interviewer emphasizes the candidate's past accomplishments. Questions posed to the candidate are intended to highlight major achievements and assess competencies, technical strengths and potential for success. The effectiveness of this technique is tied to how the question is posed and how the candidate frames his/her response. Each candidate is expected to respond to each question by giving detailed examples as proof points. In these examples he/she would outline the actions, steps, and the outcome; thereby demonstrating how his/her involvement made a difference.

Cognitive Interviews [1]

How you process information is a good predictor of
future performance

This technique uses questions that are intended to probe for aptitude and future potential. These questions are designed to be a microscope into the candidate's mind. Cognitive questions help the interviewer to better understand how the candidate thinks. For instance, is he/she a critical thinker, a problem-solver, an innovator, an analytical thinker? This technique is the best method to reveal their future potential. Cognitive interviews focus on how the candidate processes information and is ideal for evaluating his/her decision making skills. They reveal the candidate's capacity to grow and contribute meaningfully to the business beyond the role one is being hired to fill. It is a test of growth potential. As Millet notes, "Fast becoming a key metric for many hiring managers, cognitive aptitude is the ability to think, process, and react nimbly to solve problems or learn new information." (Millet, 2017)

These three (3) interviewing techniques mentioned above are usually used individually or may even be limitedly combined in each interview. Why use this approach? Why not just ask a list of set questions to test for each dimension? Does it really matter? Effectively combining all (3) three techniques provides recruiters with a three dimensional (3D) view of the candidate; the individual's professional past, personal life and potential. Using a 3D approach makes it easier for the recruiter to find the ideal candidate for the job, the brand and the business.

---

[1] If you hire an apt thinker your only responsibility is to train them to use company platforms and understand company procedures/processes. "Cognitive aptitude delivers this broad perspective, allowing companies to evaluate the long-term potential of an applicant by assessing their ability to learn quickly, adapt, and grow within a role." To properly assess the job readiness of a candidate their cognitive abilities are tested. This covers their creative thinking, problem solving, attention to details and ability to learn. A practice supported by Recruiter.com

https://www.recruiter.com/i/how-to-prove-your-cognitive-aptitude-during-a-job-interview/

What are 3 Dimensional Interviewing?

In a 3D interview the questions posed should bring out behaviors, reveal past achievements and predict future potential. While each technique on its own may be effective, each individual approach may eliminate candidates who possess high potential, and limited experience. However, by enhancing the 3D methodology with a new interviewing technique (R3 Interview Tools) interviewers will be able to identify the ideal candidate with greater precision.

As human beings, we interact and know each other on three (3) dimensions. How we think and learn about each is considered the ABC of Social Psychology. So, if we experience each other in 3D then why not hire in 3D?

Social psychology's ABCs are Affect, Behavior and Cognition

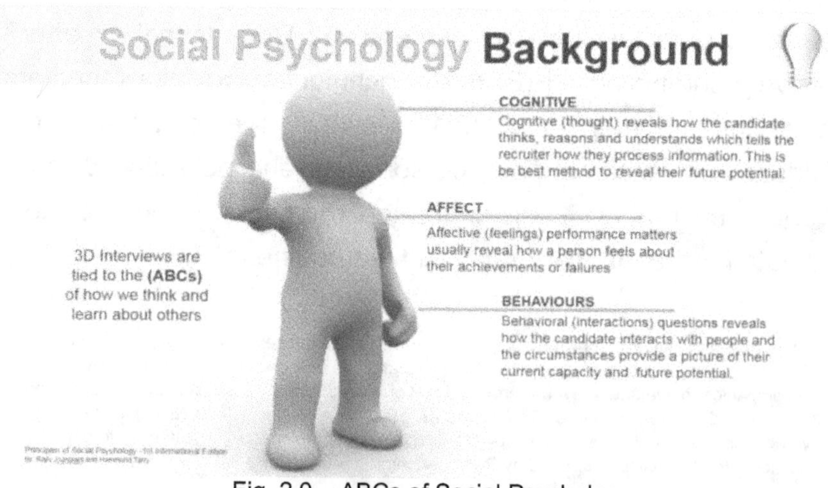

Fig. 2.0 – ABCs of Social Psychology

In order to effectively maintain and enhance our own lives through successful interaction with others, we rely on these three (3) basic and interrelated human capacities:

- **Affect** (feelings) scenarios are evidence of high or poor performance which reveal how a person feels about personal achievements or failures.

- **Behaviour** (interactions) questions indicate how the candidate interacts with people and circumstances and provide a picture of the individual's current capacity and future potential.

- **Cognition** (thought) uncovers how the candidate thinks, reasons and understands the world and this is revealed in how the individual processes information.

Internet hacks for traditional interviewing techniques are readily available online; therefore interviewers must transform the selection approach and process in order to be very effective in acquiring the BESTFIT. Interviewing candidates in a conversational and relaxed fashion should now be commonplace.

How was R3 Developed?

R3 was developed so the candidates and interviewers can enjoy the interview process. This is the reason why R3 breaks the interview down into three (3) elements. These elements help the recruiter to design each interview as an experience that is conducted with three priorities: make the candidate feel relaxed, ensure the questions asked paint a real picture of the type of person you are looking to fill the role and finally engaging the candidate with what may appear to be ridiculous exercises that help to assess their openness to change and creativity.

R3 was developed after observing interviews where highly qualified candidates were overcome with anxiety and came across as over-rehearsed. Thus they were unsuccessful. These are considered 'Bad Interviews'. Here are some of the major characteristics of a bad interview:

- The candidate is overcome by nervousness and anxiety
- The interview environment is tense
- The candidate is rehearsed and appears 'fake'
- The panel is annoyed by the rehearsed responses
- The candidate is made uncomfortable by pointless questions (e.g. what is your greatest weakness?)
- There is a belief that making the interview room high pressure would reveal the candidate's ability to operate in a high pressure environment

These six points are the model strategy for chasing away your ideal candidate and losing an opportunity for him/her to contribute meaningfully to the organizations. Recruiters should strive to:

- Make the candidate feel relaxed and set a stress-free tone for the interview

- Change the interviewing technique

- Ask questions that are realistic

R3 describes a combined approach that pulls out the main characteristics of your ideal candidate by allowing you to assess each candidate's ABCs (Affect, Behaviour and Cognition) throughout the interview.

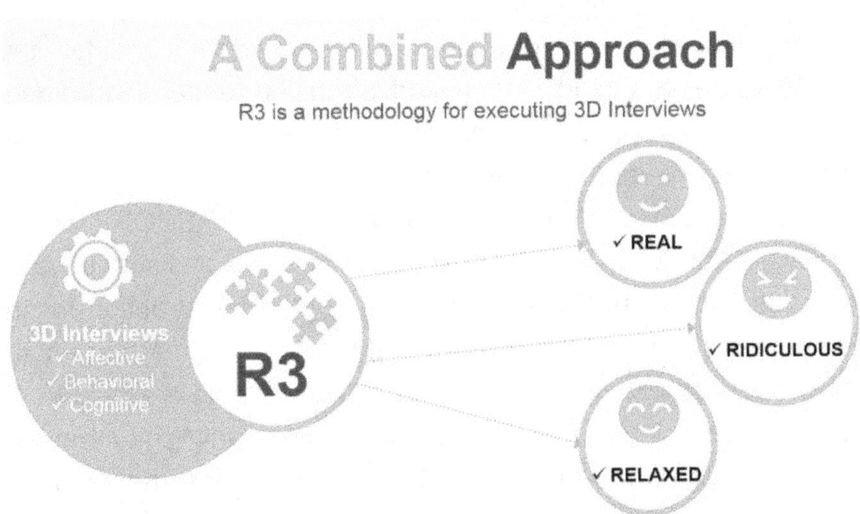

R3
Explained

Relaxed

Keep your candidate relaxed. Allow him or her to feel at peace from the moment of entry into the building.

Create a relaxed interview space. You do this because the truest version of oneself is revealed when you are relaxed and comfortable. During the interview you want to see the candidate's true self. Once the candidate enters the interview room it is the responsibility of all panelists to make this person feel comfortable in the interview space. This can include: offering water, asking about the day's activities, or favorite sports; anything to reduce and erase nervousness. Paperless interviews with folders, scoresheets and reams of paper help to remind the candidate that he/she is being 'tested' and this adds tension to the environment. Using an electronic scoresheet that interviewers can access from their phones or laptop helps to dial back the tension. However, if you decide to use printed scoresheets– DO NOT SCORE WHILE THE CANDIDATE IS SPEAKING. This is a major distraction and can add to the candidate's anxiety. It is also a distraction for the interviewers. During the interview, the panel must focus on the candidate completely. Give the interviewee time to respond to the questions and if you must score use the time while the candidate is responding to other panelists. The goal is to show the candidate that you are giving him/her your undivided attention. This will help the candidate feel that you want to hear what is being said.

The next trick is not a trick at all, listen! Spend the time listening to the candidate and even when the response misses the mark or is contrary to what you are looking for, it is important to stay in tune. While the candidate may prove to be unfit for the current role the interview performance might reveal suitability for another role. As the candidate thinks about and responds to each interview question the interviewer is able to carefully observe the candidate's ABCs (Affect, Behaviour and Cognition). As the interviewer you are only able to see this if you are present and attentive during the interview.

Real

Provide realistic scenarios and cases so that the candidate understands the context, role and culture within which he/she will be working.

Each interview is a two way conversation and assessment. The interviewer is assessing whether or not this candidate is the best fit for the role and organization; while the candidate is using the interview to assess whether or not the company and role are the desired ones. It is therefore crucial that the questions and scenarios posed to the candidate be as true to life as possible. If this interviewee will have to work on a team with a bunch of seasoned professionals who will question their authority, it is pointless to ask 'How do you manage a difficult team?' Questions like these are misleading. Use questions to paint a picture of your organization and where/how this candidate will fit into the puzzle.

Here is an example of a real question:

Organization overview: The candidate is being recruited as Manager for a team (called Team X) designed solely to look for inefficiencies in the organization. Because of this mandate this team is blamed for most redundancies. The previous manager cared very little about the team's reputation and was more focused on delivering results

Mandate: The new Manager is expected to boost team morale and change the brand reputation of Team X.

Paint a picture: You are being invited to take on the role as Manager for what the employees call Team X: the team that sends people home. However the true goal of the team is to look for inefficiencies in the organization. The current team is small and because of the stigma the employee engagement and morale among your staff is low.

Ask these questions:

1. Do you believe changing the team's reputation is important?
2. If yes why or if no why not?

3 What if you were to change the stigma and raise the employee engagement and morale of Team X, how would you achieve this?

This scenario based question paints a picture for the candidate that is realistic. It tells him/her exactly what to expect and helps the interviewer to see how this candidate will operate in the new role. Two other ways to ask the same question would be:

- If you were given a team with a poor reputation in the organization how would you change it?

- Have you ever had to work to change or build the reputation of your team?

All three (3) questions are looking for the same answers, but which would give you the candidate's ABCs (Affect, Behaviour and Cognition)?

Ridiculous

The world is changing rapidly and this requires your business to change rapidly as well; if it is to stay relevant. With this in mind using interview activities that are unusual, that is, "out of the box" and are somewhat puerile help to evaluate the candidate's ability to innovate and change.

These 'Ridiculous' interview activities are designed to allow candidates to demonstrate their cognitive aptitude. This means each activity will show the candidate's:

- Intellectual Curiosity
- Problem-Solving Skills
- Attention to Detail
- Learning Ability
- Change Management

Each activity adds whimsy to the interview while helping to lighten the mood of the interview. The outlandish nature of the activities allows the candidate to respond comfortably and the interviewers can enjoy an open conversation with the interviewee. With the activity there are no right or wrong answers, it is most beneficial when the candidate is honest and open.

As recruiters or interviewers we often struggle through our own interview process;- six candidates in and there you are asking the same questions, trying to look interested, when you realize this person is not the best fit for the role. After a long day of conducting interviews, you sometimes find yourself drained as the interviewer, and the candidates may share that they felt like the panel was disinterested in what they had to say. Having been through this experience and worse there are some questions you must ask yourself as a recruiter:

- How do you create an interview space where both the candidate and the interviewers enjoy the experience?

- How do you assess each candidate equally without having to ask the same boring questions during each interview?

Asking myself the same questions has led me to develop an interviewing technique that would help to cure the boring interview epidemic. Interviews can actually be conducted in a conversational and relaxed fashion, with tools and questions that should make the experience more pleasant for the candidates and for the interviewer, by simply using R3 Interview Tools.
R3 is based on the premise that the interview process is used to ascertain a candidate's suitability for the role and the organization; not just their aptitude, qualifications or competence. Therefore if you are hiring a lawyer, for the applicants, the

resume/CV would tell you if he/she has a law degree and the number of years of experience practicing law. The interview room is not the place to evaluate their legal expertise. Instead the interview is the place to assess if this skilled lawyer can operate effectively as an employee in your company given the environment (internal and external) within which your company operates.

When Does the Interview Begin?

For the recruiter the interview process begins the moment you make initial contact with the candidate. From that initial phone call to screen or invite them to the interview to the moment they leave the interviewing room. A good recruiter uses all these interactions to assess the candidate as a whole person. There are two levels of pre-interview assessment which I learnt from my HR Director. These would utilize two key members of any team and at the core of the company: the security guard and the receptionist. Here is how they fit in:

The Security Guard

If you are trying to achieve a friendly workspace where employees see themselves as equals and consider all members of the team valuable then start with the most invisible team member – the security guard. Allow the candidate to interact with the guard by having them sign in, collect an access pass or fill out a form. The way they treat the first ambassador of the company will reveal their true self.

The Receptionist

Once the candidate is waiting to enter the interview room the receptionist should spend time helping him/her to relax and get comfortable. Making the interview and pre-interview space comfortable and calming will help to show the best version of the candidate – their true self. It is a great way to get the candidate talking.

When the interview is over reach out to the security guard and the receptionist to hear what they have to say about the candidate's conduct and behaviour while they waited to enter the interview room. You can also create a brief feedback survey instrument and have them fill it out after interacting with each candidate.
If the interview is conducted elsewhere (e.g. a restaurant) then speak with the maître D' or the most appropriate person.

Dive Into the Ridiculous: Interview Activities

When using each activity, note that this kit is designed for the interviewer to evaluate each candidate in a 3D fashion during the interview process. This means paying attention to the candidate's ABCs (Affect, Behaviour and Cognition). It is also important to maintain a relaxed environment and only pose real questions. Before introducing the activity paint a picture for the candidate of the type of organization/team/department they will be working in and the present state of the organization (growing/evolving/dying/re-inventing/restructuring and so on).

Puzzled

Activity 1.0 - Puzzled

Instructions

This tool is ideal for roles that require multi-tasking. Ask the candidate to speak on a topic with which he/she is very comfortable with or an achievement that evokes excitement

While the interviewee is speaking, request the completion of a simple puzzle with some information about your organization. (e.g. tagline or core values)

OBSERVATIONS

The aim of this activity is not to find the candidate who can talk while piecing together a puzzle. Instead, your focus should be on how each candidate works. Look out for:

1. Candidates who pause to complete the puzzle before or after answering the question.

2. Observe the candidate's attention to details; did he/she focus heavily on ensuring the pieces fit perfectly or was understanding what the puzzle pieces created more important to the candidate?

3. At the end of the activity, is the candidate able to tell you what was on the puzzle when you took it away? Was he/she paying attention to what was written on the puzzle or was he/she simply going through the motions?

Use these observations to evaluate the ABCs you need for this role. (E.g. A multitasker with keen attention to details.)

One of These Things is Not Like The Other

Activity 2.0 – One of These Things is not Like the Other

Instructions

On the table place 2 sets of items (e.g. pencils and folder clips). Ensure that the pencils have clear differences. Break the point of one and slot it back in place. Next do the same with the eraser of another pencil. Ensure that these defects are not visible at first glance

Ask the candidate to examine the item carefully. That is, touch it, pick it up and do whatever is deemed necessary to provide a full assessment. Then ask:

1. If you were asked to inspect and evaluate the quality of these items what defects or issues would you state in your report

OBSERVATIONS

The aim of this activity is not to find the candidate who can identify the defective pencil quickly or any superficial flaws like colour and a broken point. Pay attention to the following:

1. Once the candidate receives the instructions, is there a probe to establish what is your baseline or standard (what is a defect or what is quality)?

2. When inspecting the items, does the candidate try using each item (e.g. did he/she try writing with the pencil?)

3. In his/her response does the candidate make any recommendations for resolving or remedying the defects?

Use these observations to evaluate the ABCs you need for this role. (E.g. A auditor/investigator with the ability to monitor policy, identify breaches and make recommendations.)

Set in Stone

Activity 3.0 – Set In Stone

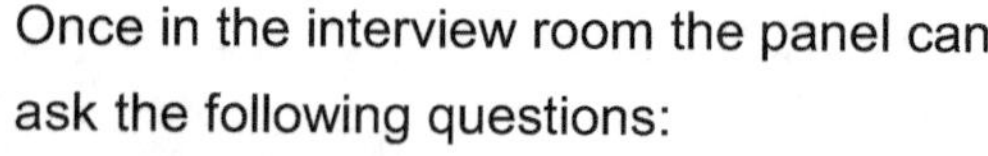

Instructions

Before entering the interview room present each candidate with a marker and a basket of rocks. Ask him/her to write on the stone what value or principle for them is set in stone. This is something they would not require compromise on.
The candidate can write on one or multiple stones, no limitations.

Once in the interview room the panel can ask the following questions:

1. What did you think of the activity?
2. Explain why this is set in stone for you?
3. What does this say about you as a leader?

OBSERVATIONS

The aim of this activity is not to find the candidate who has too many or too few things set in stone. This is not a test of the candidate's flexibility. Pay attention to the following:

1. Once the candidate is given the initial instructions, what is the reaction to the activity, is the activity regarded as ridiculous or silly?

2. Listen keenly to what the candidate says throughout the interview, make note of moments when the value(s) or principle(s) that he/she wrote do not line-up with their responses.

3. Assess how well the candidate embraces the activity and the ease with which there is full engagement.

Use these observations to evaluate the ABCs you need for this role. (E.g. A leader who values integrity will demonstrate integrity in his/her personal and professional life)

Grapes of Wrath

Activity 4.0 – Grapes of Wrath

Instructions

Your candidate may have to interact with employees, customers and leader who are angry from time to time. Their responses to anger or frustration can either create tension or remove tension in the workplace.

Invite the candidate to pick a grape from
each grape vine and explain their strategy
to address each issue

Angry Staff

Angry Staff usually have the following issues:

- Disengagement
- Lack of tools & resources
- Compensation
- Fulfilment

Angry Customers

Angry Customers usually have the following issues:

- Long wait times
- Poor Service
- Inferior Products/Service
- Misleading information

Angry Supervisor

Angry Supervisors usually have the following issues:

- Lazy Staff
- Lack of tools & resources
- Lack of direction or clear instructions
- Unrealistic targets

You're Angry

You're Angry because of the following issues:

- Lack of tools & resources
- Misleading information
- Unrealistic targets
- Workplace Tension

OBSERVATIONS

The aim of this activity is not to find the candidate with the best or most practical solution as most of the solution strategies are straight forward. Instead your aim is to observe how the candidate uses practical or text book solutions while demonstrating emotional intelligence. This is not a test of the candidate's ingenuity. Pay attention to the following:

1. Once the candidate is given the initial instructions, what is the reaction to the activity, is the activity regarded as ridiculous or silly?

2. Once the candidate receives the instructions is there a probe to establish what the culture of the organization is or is there reference to a specific example

3. Are the questions answered with an 'us vs them' mode of speaking

4. Does the candidate pay attention to some anger issues over other anger issues?

Use these observations to evaluate the ABCs you need for this role. (E.g. A leader who is emotionally intelligent will see all anger issues as worth addressing, as they impact productivity)

Building your Ideal Team

Activity 5.0 – Building Your Ideal Team

Instructions

Indicate to the candidate that he/she may
be required to engage in building a team.
Using these 6 employees they need to identity the following:

- Who do you want on your team? (and why?)

- Who do you not want on your team?
(and why)

- Next ask the candidate to select 2 team members to remove from the team

- At the end of the interview ask the candidate to indicate which team member is most like him/her

Mr.Frank the Fanatic

For this employee everything is in crisis mode and the sky is always falling. He works well under pressure and delivers high quality results.

Mr.Larry the Lazy

Lazy and resourceful, this employee is always looking for the easiest way to complete any task.

Mr.Jack of all Trades

Jack of all trades and everybody's helper. This employee is extremely helpful and often gets sidetracked from his core functions due to his helpful nature

Ms.Joy the Fanatic

Joy is the comedian of the group who keeps everyone smiling. She makes everyone feel comfortable in awkward situations but spends little time doing her job

Ms.Caren the Confidential

Confidential, committed and very ambitious. She is on the side of anyone who is in charge.

Ms.Melissa the Militant

Militant and business-like, this employee is strict. She works to rule and allows little room for flexibility. She has only one interest- doing what she is paid to do and doing it well.

OBSERVATIONS

With this activity there is no right or wrong answer. The aim of this activity is to assess the candidate's ability to work with and lead a diverse team, while demonstrating leadership traits, how he/she view himself/herself as a leader and team member. Pay attention to the following:

1. Does the candidate's ideal team closely reflect the personalities in the actual team he/she will be leading or working with?

2. Is the candidate able to identify the strengths in the different personalities and build on them to get maximum benefit for the team (e.g. Larry is Lazy but resourceful)?

3. Does the candidate read through the descriptions thoroughly or does the candidate overlook key elements of the team members' personalities?

4. When asked to let go 2 or more team members how does the candidate respond to this request (probe, push back or follow blindly?

5. Once the interview is over, ask the candidate which team member best describes or matches his/her personality. Did the candidate choose to remove himself/herself from the team?

Use these observations to evaluate the ABCs you need for this role. (E.g. A leader who is able to develop his/her team, therefore seeing the potential in working with Larry and Frank)

The Un-Official Leader

Activity 6.0 – The Un-Official Leader

Instructions

Every team has an unofficial leader. As a complement to the activity above invite the candidate to pick a name out of a hat. Explain that the name selected represents a member of the team who represents its informal leader.

Ask the candidate to identify the potential conflicts they see arising from having this person on the team and to explain strategies to address, solve, manage or respond to this 'issue'.

The Advocate

Anti-management and leadership this employee is a leader with a wealth of knowledge.

The Ghost of Bosses Past

Always living in the past this employee compares you to other leaders who are long gone. He/She is quite averse to change and refuses to step into the 21st century.

The Overlooked Leader

Passed over for the post you now hold this employee has a bag of sour grapes. There may not be any deliberate sabotage of your work, but this individual inadvertently will create tension on the team

The Undercover Boss

Hardly ever has anything to say publicly, but is always ready to spread gossip on the team. Operates like a spy and undermines all effort to change, improve or develop the team

The Terrorist

Using intimidation, this employee is extremely aggressive and short tempered. Behaves in a manner that makes other members of the team uncomfortable and will cause intense squabbles with some members of the team.

Mr. Cold Water

Also considered a pessimist this employee never has a positive word to say about any changes or success. This person will inundate the team with reasons why any solution or idea is not good enough, won't work or is a waste of time

OBSERVATIONS

The aim of this activity is to observe how the candidate uses practical or text book solutions while demonstrating emotional intelligence. This is a test of the candidate's ingenuity and influence. Pay attention to the following:

1. Once the candidate receives the instructions is there a probe to establish what the culture of the team is or is there an attempt to get ask the panel to reference a specific example?

2. Does the candidate make an effort to validate or understand the status, feelings or background of the informal leader?

3. Does the candidate convey a plan that is combative or collaborative?

Use these observations to evaluate the ABCs you need for this role. (E.g. A leader who is charismatic for a team that has a lot of baggage/tension)

Is R3 Right for You?

R3 is a good tool for any recruiter, however the stage your business is at, will impact the effectiveness of the technique. To know if this tool is ideal for your company, do an evaluation. Your first question is "What is your relationship with change?"

If your team or company is averse to change and not open to risk taking then R3 might not be a suitable model for your business. When hiring you do not want to recruit a maverick (which represents the BESTFIT for where you see the company/ department in the next 3 years) when you really need a conformist (who represents your current state). Remember the interview process is about identifying the candidate who is the BESTFIT for the role, team and company (in that order of priority).

Employing a maverick for a team that is led by a conformist will frustrate both employees. How do you avoid this? As the recruiter, you must evaluate the business needs, the team's needs in relation to the company's current state and future state. This evaluation will help to determine if this model is for you.

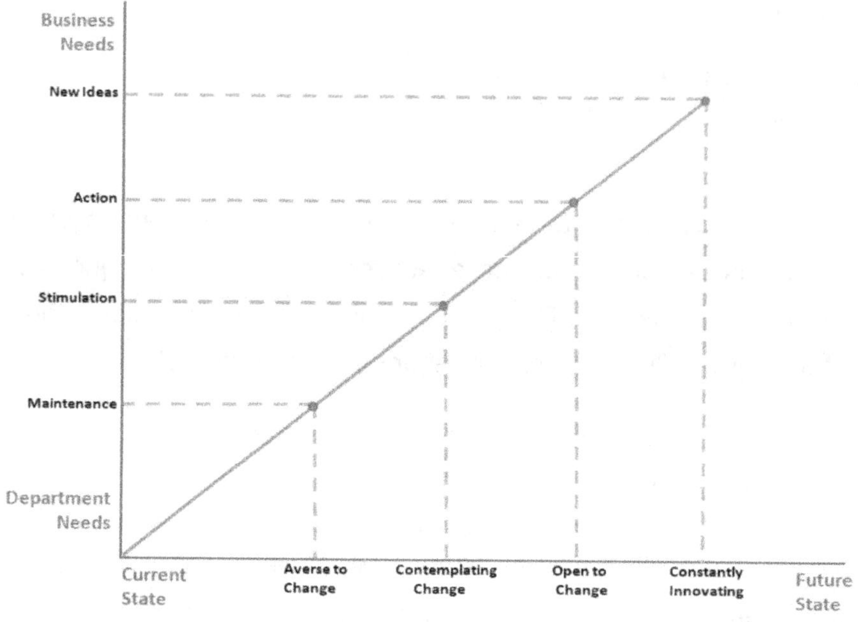

A company that is averse to change is unlikely to have a department that is interested in hiring an employee who is an innovator and full of new ideas. That innovator will frustrate both self and the team. The chart above demonstrates when and how to know the state of the business (e.g. open to change). The next step is to look at the impact of the role on the organization (e.g. the priority of this role in the department; which needs stimulation). This means you will need to hire someone who will stimulate change in the department and drive (action) change in the organization.

To put it simply the R3 technique is ideal for organizations recruiting for transition from one state to the next or a business that is constantly innovating and changing. If your business is averse to change and is seeking to employ someone to maintain the status-quo this model is not for you.

As a recruiter you do not have to pull out this book to assess if the model is right for you each time you prepare for an interview. Instead you can do a simple mental check or use the table below and ensure that you are at the top of the box. The Xs here paint a picture of where you want to be with your recruitment if you are planning to use R3. For this chart simply mark an 'X' next to the box that best reflects where this role fits in.

BUSINESS NEEDS	New Ideas	X	X	Innovating	FUTURE STATE
	Action			Open To Change	
	Stimulation	X	X	Contemplating Change	
DEPARTMENT NEEDS	Maintenance			Averse To Change	CURRENT STATE

Combining the Rs (R3) will help you, the recruiter, to identify the candidate who is best suited for the role and is closely aligned to the organization.

The change you are embarking on has to be planned and strategic. This means R3 can help when making strategic hires at any level of the organization when starting or in the middle of a planned change programme. Using this model cannot be a knee jerk reaction or a one off recruitment activity. It would be unwise to cherry pick elements of the tool (e.g. a tense interview with ridiculous activities) as it adversely impacts the outcome. R3 is not a quick fix or a cure all, but is designed to be used as a part of a comprehensive recruitment strategy.

Conclusion

The R3 technique carries four (4) clear benefits:

- *Behavioral interviews that are conducted in a conversational and relaxed fashion will allow the candidate to reveal his/her true self*

- *It is harder to trick or train for these interview tools. There is most likely no answer that is right or wrong. The value placed on the candidate's responses is based on what the recruiter is looking for*

- *This method evaluates all sides of the candidate; personality, skill, performance legacy and aptitude*

- *Organizations change and so do people. These tools are good predictors of future behaviour potential*

Making this technique the linchpin for your recruitment strategy will be an ideal precursor to a dynamic professional development strategy and robust leadership development programme.

I have used these tools, shared them with colleagues and the response from both the candidates and interviewers have been the same. The candidates felt fulfilled during the interview and relaxed; while the interviewer enjoyed the interview process from the first to the last candidate. One candidate said to me in a post interview discussion that "after being in the interview I knew I wasn't the right fit for the job. I am qualified, but I wasn't what you were looking for and that job wasn't for me".

Here are some other comments for both candidates and recruiters:

"R3 doesn't only interview your
intellect, it interviews the whole
person"
~ Tania (HR Director)

"The tool was a good way to get important insights."
~ Shoshanna (Recruiter)

"I knew there was no right or wrong answer,
so the interview felt relaxed"
~ Dane (Candidate)

This technique provides a platform for the candidate to showcase he/she strongest attributes and potential beyond what is shared in their CV or resume. He/She can paint a picture of himself/herself in the context of the role and organization. The aim is not to win over the panel, but to prove to each interviewer that his/her is the **BESTFIT** for the job.

References

Edison Questions Stir Up A Storm. (1921, May 11). The New York Times, p.
        https://timesmachine.nytimes.com/timesmachine/1921/05/11/98685607.
        pdf.

Jonge, T. d. (2015, September 4). Getting with the times, Giving Old-
School Interview Questions a Modern Twist.
        Retrieved from LinkedIn: https://www.linkedin.com/pulse/getting-
        times-giving-old-school-interview-questionsmodern-de-jonge/

Kellaway, L. (2012, October 7). The question with interviews is why we bother
        Retrieved from Financial Times:
        https://www.ft.com/content/4d84475e-0e46-11e2-b87e-00144feabdc0

Millet, J. (2017, October 26). How to Prove Your Cognitive Aptitude During a Job
        Interview. Retrieved from Recruiter.com: https://www.recruiter.com/i/
        how-to-prove-your-cognitive-aptitude-during-a-job-interview/

Patrick Hauenstein, P. (2014, November 19). A Brief History of the
        Employment Interview. Retrieved from
        theomniview.com: http://www.theomniview.com/pov/blog/a-
        brief-history-of-the-employment-interview/

Performance Based Interview Questions: Everything You Need to Know. (n.d.).
        Retrieved from UpCounsel:
        https://www.upcounsel.com/performance-based-interview-questions

Reed, S. M. (2017). A Guide to the Human Resource Body of Knowledge.
        Hoboken, New Jersey: John Wiley & Sons, Inc.

Tarry, R. J. (2014). Principles of Social Psychology - 1st International Edition.
        Creative Commons Attribution 4.0 International License.

The HeadHunters. (2014). Going for a Job Interview: Old School vs New School.
        Vancouver, Canada. Retrieved from theheadhunters.ca.

Wasserman, N. (2000, March 1). A Closer Look at Behavior-Based
        Interviewing.   Retrieved   from   inc.com:
        https://www.inc.com/articles/2000/03/17957. html

Wolfe, B. (2015). The Little Black Book of Human Resources Management. The
        Expressive Press

BestFit The

Rochelle Analecia Reid James is a selfless individual whose life's mission is to create and advance ideas that will give others a sense of self-worth and uplift human existence.
She is a multi-faceted professional who has the uncanny ability to unearth hidden talents in others. It is this character trait that has prompted her to seek ways of abandoning the mundane interviewing techniques and introducing a model that will ensure that competent and qualified applicants are not dismissed by unimaginative interviewers.

Rochelle has the remarkable ability to identify geniuses shrouded in fear and intimidation, and stifled by the absence of confidence. She presents an uncomplicated method of detecting competence and leadership traits. This book encapsulates Rochelle's dream to ensure that talents are not overlooked because of the inability to articulate 'rehearsed' responses at an interview.

The writing style is witty, but not whimsical, profound without being pedantic. This book is captivating and engenders great excitement as the model unfolds. This great writer erodes age and status barriers, creating a master piece that leaves the interviewer eager to attempt this technique, and the interviewee anxious to meet an interviewer who practices this model.

By Pauleen Reid

9 789769 633100